To Chris

From Jim

D1006259

Mark
TWAIN

Wit
AND
Wisecracks

Selected by Doris Benardete

Photographs from Corbis-Bettmann

PETER PAUPER PRESS, INC.
WHITE PLAINS, NEW YORK

The sayings in this book are taken from the various works of Mark Twain and are reprinted by permission of Harper & Brothers.

Copyright ©1998
Peter Pauper Press, Inc.
202 Mamaroneck Avenue
White Plains, NY 10601
All rights reserved
ISBN 978-0-88088-080-0
Printed in China
28 27 26 25 24 23

Visit us at peterpauper.com

Mark
TWAIN

Wit
AND
Wisecracks

Twain (ca. 1902) visiting his home in Hannibal, Missouri

Let us be thankful for the fools. But for them the rest of us could not succeed.

It's better to keep your mouth shut and appear stupid than to open it and remove all doubt.

Adam was but human—this explains it all. He did not want the apple for the apple's sake, he wanted it only because it was forbidden. The mistake was in not forbidding the serpent; then he would have eaten the serpent.

I believe that our Heavenly Father
invented man because he was
disappointed in the monkey.

History is better than prophecy.
In fact history is prophecy. And
history says that whenever a weak
and ignorant people possess a thing
which a strong and enlightened
people want, it must be yielded
up peaceably.

I never could tell a lie that anybody
would doubt, nor a truth that anybody would believe.

The way it is now, the asylums can hold the sane people, but if we tried to shut up the insane we should run out of building materials.

Adam and Eve had many advantages, but the principal one was that they escaped teething.

Emotions are among the toughest things in the world to manufacture out of whole cloth: it is easier to manufacture seven facts than one emotion.

The difference between the right
word and the almost right word
is the difference between lightning
and the lightning bug.

I have long ago lost my belief in
immortality—also my interest
in it.

By trying, we can easily learn to
endure adversity. Another man's,
I mean.

When angry, count four; when very angry, swear.

Whoever has lived long enough to find out what life is knows how deep a debt of gratitude we owe to Adam, the first great benefactor of our race. He brought death into the world.

Classic: A book which people praise and don't read.

His ignorance covered the whole earth like a blanket and there was hardly a hole in it anywhere.

Eternal Rest sounds comforting in the pulpit. . . . Well, you try it once, and see how heavy time will hang on your hands.

Happiness ain't a *thing in itself*—it's only a *contrast* with something that ain't pleasant.

Man is the only animal that blushes. Or needs to.

Grief can take care of itself; but to get the full value of a joy you must have somebody to divide it with.

War talk by men who have been in a war is always interesting; whereas moon talk by a poet who has not been in the moon is likely to be dull.

Everything human is pathetic. The secret source of humor itself is not joy but sorrow. There is no humor in heaven.

There is no family in America without a clock, and consequently there is no fair pretext for the usual Sunday medley of dreadful sounds that issues from our steeples.

I could have become a soldier myself if I had waited. I had got part of it learned; I knew more about retreating than the man that invented retreating.

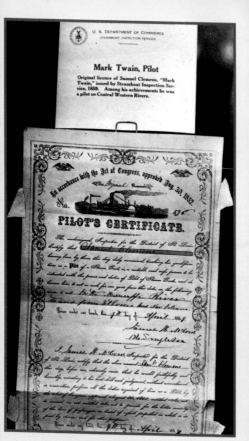

The Steamboat Pilot's Certificate granted to Samuel Clemens (a.k.a. Mark Twain) in April, 1859

Nothing so needs reforming as other people's habits.

His face was as blank as a target after a militia shooting-match.

Thunder is good, thunder is impressive; but it is lightning that does the work.

Good breeding consists in concealing how much we think of ourselves and how little we think of the other person.

A sin takes on new and real terrors when there seems a chance that it is going to be found out.

Don't part with your illusions. When they are gone you may still exist but you have ceased to live.

If the desire to kill and the opportunity to kill came always together, who would escape hanging?

It can be no sufficient compensation to a corpse to know that the dynamite that laid him out was not of as good a quality as it had been supposed to be.

Figures often beguile me, particularly when I have the arranging of them myself; in which case the remark attributed to Disraeli would often apply with justice and force: "There are three kinds of lies: lies, damned lies and statistics."

A soap bubble is the most beautiful thing, and the most exquisite, in nature.

April 1. This is the day upon which we are reminded of what we are on the other three hundred and sixty-four.

When whole races and peoples conspire to propagate gigantic mute lies in the interest of tyrannies and shams, why should we care anything about the trifling lies told by individuals?

In the first place God made idiots. This was for practice. Then He made School Boards.

Thousands of geniuses live and die undiscovered—either by themselves or by others.

When red-headed people are above a certain social grade their hair is auburn.

Whenever the literary German dives into a sentence, that is the last you are going to see of him till he emerges on the other side of his Atlantic with his verb in his mouth.

I knew that in Biblical times if a man committed a sin the extermination of the whole surrounding nation— cattle and all—was likely to happen. I knew that Providence was not particular about the rest, so that He got somebody connected with the one He was after.

He didn't utter a word, but he exuded mute blasphemy from every pore.

The principal difference between a cat and a lie is that a cat has only nine lives.

It takes your enemy and your friend, working together, to hurt you to the heart: the one to slander you and the other to get the news to you.

To succeed in the other trades, capacity must be shown; in the law, concealment of it will do.

We have a criminal jury system which is superior to any in the world and its efficiency is only marred by the difficulty of finding twelve men every day who don't know anything and can't read.

The author, age 55, posing for a portrait with top hat

Let us endeavor so to live that when we come to die even the undertaker will be sorry.

Truth is good manners; manners are a fiction.

When a person cannot deceive himself the chances are against his being able to deceive other people.

It is a pity that we cannot escape from life when we are young.

We haven't all had the good fortune to be ladies; we haven't all been generals, or poets, or statesmen; but when the toast works down to the babies, we stand on common ground.

I am no lazier now than I was forty years ago, but that is because I reached the limit forty years ago. You can't go beyond possibility.

He is useless on top of the ground;
he ought to be under it, inspiring
the cabbages.

You can't depend on your eyes when
your imagination is out of focus.

He died two years ago of over-
cerebration. He was a poor sort of a
creature and by nature and training
a fraud. As a liar he was well enough
and had some success but no
distinction.

It takes some little time to accept and realize the fact that while you have been growing old, your friends have not been standing still.

Against a diseased imagination demonstration goes for nothing.

Habit is habit, and not to be flung out of the window by any man, but coaxed downstairs a step at a time.

"America's best known humorist" had already published Huckleberry Finn *and* Innocents Abroad *when he was the subject of this caricature by Joseph Keppler, ca. 1885.*

We despise all reverences and all the objects of reverence which are outside the pale of our own list of sacred things. And yet, with strange inconsistency, we are shocked when other people despise and defile the things which are holy to us.

You aim for the palace and get drowned in the sewer.

It isn't what sum you get, it's how much you can buy with it, that's the important thing; and it's that that tells whether your wages are high in fact or only high in name.

I thoroughly disapprove of duels.
I consider them unwise and I know
they are dangerous. Also, sinful.
If a man should challenge me
now I would go to that man and
take him kindly and forgivingly by
the hand and lead him to a quiet
retired spot and *kill* him.

I was seldom able to see an opportunity until it had ceased to be one.

We can secure other people's
approval, if we do right and try hard;
but our own is worth a hundred of
it, and no way has been found of
securing that.

There are several good protections against temptation: but the surest is cowardice.

We have not the reverent feeling for the rainbow that the savage has, because we know how it is made. We have lost as much as we gained by prying into that matter.

It was ever thus, all through my life: whenever I have diverged from custom and principle and uttered a truth, the rule has been that the hearer hadn't strength of mind enough to believe it.

There are people who strictly deprive themselves of each and every eatable, drinkable and smokable which has in any way acquired a shady reputation. They pay this price for health. And health is all they get. How strange it is!

When a teacher calls a boy by his entire name it means trouble.

A crime persevered in a thousand centuries ceases to be a crime, and becomes a virtue.

It is sound judgment to put on a bold face and play your hand for a hundred times what it is worth; forty-nine times out of fifty nobody dares to "call," and you roll in the chips.

In Paris they just simply opened their eyes and stared when we spoke to them in French! We never did succeed in making those idiots understand their own language.

Training is everything. The peach was once a bitter almond; cauliflower is nothing but cabbage with a college education.

It is not worth while to strain one's self to tell the truth to people who habitually discount everything you tell them, whether it is true or isn't.

One mustn't criticize other people on grounds where he can't stand per-pendicular himself.

The rich don't care for anybody but themselves; it's only the poor that have feeling for the poor, and help them.

Twain (ca. 1905) sitting in an easy chair in his Hartford, Connecticut home

In true beauty, more depends
upon right location and judicious
distribution of feature than upon
multiplicity of them. So also as
regards color. The very combination
of colors which in a volcanic irrup-
tion would add beauty to a landscape
might detach it from a girl.

He had no principles and was
delightful company.

Often it does seem such a pity that
Noah and his party did not miss the
boat.

Whenever we have a strong and persistent and ineradicable instinct we may be sure that it is not original with us but inherited—inherited from away back and hardened and perfected by the petrifying influence of time.

Work consists of whatever a body is *obliged* to do, and Play consists of whatever a body is not obliged to do.

Truth *is* stranger than Fiction, but it is because Fiction is obliged to stick to possibilities; Truth isn't.

The 74-year-old Twain at his billiard table

Carlyle said "a lie cannot live." It shows that he did not know how to tell them.

When I was younger I could remember anything, whether it had happened or not; but my faculties are decaying now and soon I shall be so I cannot remember any but the things that never happened. It is sad to go to pieces like this but we all have to do it.

Few slanders can stand the wear of silence.

All war must be just . . . the killing of strangers against whom you feel no personal animosity; strangers whom, in other circumstances, you would help if you found them in trouble, and who would help you if you needed it.

There comes a time in every rightly-constructed boy's life when he has a raging desire to go somewhere and dig for hidden treasure.

The man who is born stingy can be taught to give liberally—with his hands; but not with his heart.

We must put up with our clothes as they are—they have their reason for existing. They are on us to expose us—to advertise what we wear them to conceal. They are a sign; a sign of insincerity; a sign of suppressed vanity; a pretense that we desire gorgeous colors and the graces of harmony and form; and we put them on to propagate that lie and back it up.

The timid man yearns for full value, and asks a tenth; the bold man strikes for double value, and compromises at par.

No brute ever does a cruel thing—
that is the monopoly of those with
the moral sense. When a brute inflicts
pain he does it innocently; it is not
wrong; for him there is no such thing
as wrong. And he does not inflict
pain for the pleasure of inflicting it—
only man does that.

The very ink with which all history is
written is merely fluid prejudice.

The highest perfection of politeness
is only a beautiful edifice, built, from
the base to the dome, of graceful and
gilded forms of charitable and
unselfish lying.

There is an old-time toast which is golden for its beauty: "When you ascend the hill of prosperity may you not meet a friend."

It is by the goodness of God that in our country we have those three unspeakably precious things: freedom of speech, freedom of conscience, and the prudence never to practice either of them.

My mother had a great deal of trouble with me but I think she enjoyed it.

There is nothing in the world like a persuasive speech to fuddle the mental apparatus and upset the convictions and debauch the emotions of an audience not practiced in the tricks and delusions of oratory.

What are the proper proportions of a maxim? A minimum of sound to a maximum of sense.

Let me make the superstitions of a nation and I care not who makes its laws or its songs either.

Why is it that we rejoice at a birth and grieve at a funeral? It is because we are not the person involved.

All say, "How hard it is that we have to die"—a strange complaint to come from the mouths of people who have had to live.

Few things are harder to put up with than the annoyance of a good example.

Let us not be too particular. It is better to have old second-hand diamonds than none at all.

I was gratified to be able to answer promptly, and I did. I said I didn't know.

It could probably be shown by facts and figures that there is no distinctly native American criminal class except Congress.

Truth is the most valuable thing we have. Let us economize it.

In these latter days it seems hard to realize that there was ever a time when the robbing of our government was a novelty.

We adore titles and heredities in our hearts and ridicule them with our mouths. This is our democratic privilege.

Each boy has one or two sensitive spots and if you can find out where they are located you have only to touch them and you can scorch him as with fire.

Forget and forgive. This is not difficult, when properly understood. It means that you are to forget inconvenient duties, and forgive yourself for forgetting. In time, by rigid practice and stern determination, it comes easy.

He imagined that he was in love with her, whereas I think she did the imagining for him.

Any mummery will cure if the patient's faith is strong in it.

But in my age, as in my youth, night brings me many a deep remorse. I realize that from the cradle up I have been like the rest of the race—never quite sane in the night.

Each person is born to one possession which outvalues all his others—his last breath.

I have criticized absent people so often, and then discovered, to my humiliation, that I was talking with their relatives, that I have grown superstitious about that sort of thing and dropped it.

The proverb says that Providence protects children and idiots. This is really true. I know it because I have tested it.

If you pick up a starving dog and make him prosperous, he will not bite you. This is the principal difference between a dog and a man.

A man pretty much always refuses another man's first offer, no matter what it is.

The government of my country snubs
honest simplicity, but fondles artistic
villainy, and I think I might have
developed into a very capable pick-
pocket if I had remained in the public
service a year or two.

Man will do many things to get himself loved; he will do all things to get
himself envied.

We were little Christian children and
had early been taught the value of
forbidden fruit.

Twain with his pen and cigars close at hand

Beautiful credit! The foundation of modern society. Who shall say that this is not the golden age of mutual trust, of unlimited reliance upon human promises?

Sage-brush is very fair fuel, but as a vegetable it is a distinguished failure. Nothing can abide the taste of it, but the jackass and his illegitimate child, the mule.

There are times when one would like to hang the whole human race and finish the farce.

No country can be well governed
unless its citizens as a body keep reli-
giously before their minds that they
are the guardians of the law, and that
the law officers are only the machin-
ery for its execution, nothing more.

I have witnessed and greatly enjoyed
the first act of everything which
Wagner created, but the effect on me
has always been so powerful that one
act was quite sufficient; whenever I
have witnessed two acts I have gone
away physically exhausted; and whenever I have ventured an entire opera
the result has been the next thing to
suicide.

After all these years, I see that I was mistaken about Eve in the beginning; it is better to live outside the Garden with her than inside it without her.

Consider well the proportion of things. It is better to be a young June-bug than an old bird of paradise.

There are people who think that honesty is always the best policy. This is a superstition; there are times when the appearance of it is worth six of it.

No people in the world ever did achieve their freedom by goody-goody talk and moral suasion: it being immutable law that all revolutions that will succeed must *begin* in blood, whatever may answer afterward.

There are those who scoff at the schoolboy, calling him frivolous and shallow. Yet it was the schoolboy who said, "Faith is believing what you know ain't so."

Every one is a moon, and has a dark side which he never shows to anybody.

It is easy to find fault, if one has that
disposition. There was once a man
who, not being able to find any other
fault with his coal, complained that
there were too many prehistoric
toads in it.

Reverence for one's own sacred
things—parents, religion, flag,
laws, and respect for one's own
beliefs—these are feelings which we
cannot even help. They come natural
to us; they are involuntary, like
breathing. There is no personal merit
in breathing.

Always do right. This will gratify some people, and astonish the rest.

The calm confidence of a Christian with four aces.

It is more trouble to make a maxim than it is to do right.

If you should rear a duck in the heart of the Sahara, no doubt it would swim if you brought it to the Nile.

*Twain looking out of the window from the den
of his Elmira, New York residence*

Wrinkles should merely indicate where the smiles have been.

Custom is a petrifaction; nothing but dynamite can dislodge it for a century.

Many a small thing has been made large by the right kind of advertising.

When you are expecting the worst, you get something that is not so bad, after all.

When I reflect upon the number of disagreeable people who I know have gone to a better world, I am moved to lead a different life.

Its name is Public Opinion. It is held in reverence. It settles everything. Some think it is the voice of God.

The *can-can*. The idea of it is to dance as wildly, as noisily, as furiously as you can; expose yourself as much as possible if you are a woman; and kick as high as you can, no matter which sex you belong to.

He was as shy as a newspaper is when referring to its own merits.

If the man doesn't believe as we do, we say he is a crank, and that settles it. I mean it does nowadays, because we can't burn him.

The man who is ostentatious of his modesty is twin to the statue that wears a fig-leaf.

If there is one thing that will make a man peculiarly and insufferably self-conceited, it is to have his stomach behave itself, the first day at sea, when nearly all his comrades are seasick.

When a person of mature age perpetrates a practical joke it is fair evidence, I think, that he is weak in the head and hasn't enough heart to signify.

We ought never to do wrong when people are looking.

Schoolboy days are no happier than the days of after life, but we look back upon them regretfully because we have forgotten our punishments at school, and how we grieved when our marbles were lost and our kites destroyed—because we have forgotten all the sorrows and privations of that canonized epoch and remember only its orchard robberies, its wooden sword pageants, and its fishing holidays.

I have noticed my conscience for many years, and I know it is more trouble and bother to me than anything else I started with.

To be the *first*—that is the idea.
To do something, say something,
see something, before *anybody*
else—these are the things that confer
a pleasure compared with which
other pleasures are tame and com-
monplace, other ecstasies cheap
and trivial.

Every man is a suffering-machine and
a happiness-machine combined. The
two functions work together harmoni-
ously, with a fine and delicate preci-
sion on the give-and-take principle.
For every happiness turned out in the
one department the other stands
ready to modify it with a sorrow or a
pain—maybe a dozen.

Death, the only immortal who treats us all alike, whose pity and whose peace and whose refuge are for all—the soiled and the pure, the rich and the poor, the loved and the unloved.

I wish there was something in that miserable spiritualism, so we could send them word.

The reports of my death are greatly exaggerated.